# GOLD
## *ON*
# GOLD

The Essential Guide To Hedge
Against The Great Financial Reset

### R. E. GOLD

Birchwood DRIVE Publishing
Craryville, New York

Copyright © 2026 by 925Thrift LLC
All rights reserved.

No part of this book may be reproduced, stored in a retrieval system, or transmitted in any form or by any means; electronic, mechanical, photocopying, recording, or otherwise without prior written permission of the publisher, except for brief quotations in printed reviews.

First Edition, 2026

Paperback ISBN: 979-8-9942893-0-3
eBook ISBN: 979-8-9942893-1-0

Disclaimer:

The information contained in this book is provided for educational and informational purposes only and should not be construed as financial, investment, legal, or tax advice. 925Thrift LLC, the publisher, and the author make no representations, warranties, or guarantees regarding the accuracy, completeness, or reliability of any information, commentary, analysis, opinions, or recommendations contained herein. Readers are solely responsible for their own financial decisions.

You should always consult a qualified financial professional and conduct your own independent research and due diligence before making any investment or financial decision. To the maximum extent permitted by law, the publisher and the author disclaim any and all liability for any loss, risk, or damages whether direct, indirect, incidental, or consequential arising from the use of, or reliance upon, the information presented in this book. Past performance, historical examples, and illustrative scenarios are not guarantees of future results.

# Table of Contents

World Debt and Global Concerns ............................................... 1

Why Gold ............................................................................. 7

Properties of Gold ................................................................. 15

Treasure Hunt ...................................................................... 25

Be Your Own Bank ............................................................... 35

Gold vs Silver ....................................................................... 45

The End Game ..................................................................... 55

Nuggets ............................................................................... 63

R&R .................................................................................... 71

Terminology ......................................................................... 75

Appendix ............................................................................. 83

Acknowledgments ................................................................ 85

About the Author .................................................................. 87

*"But then finally the masses wake up.
They become suddenly aware of the fact that inflation is
a deliberate policy and will go on endlessly. A breakdown
occurs. The crack-up boom appears. Everybody is anxious
to swap his money against "real" goods, no matter whether
he need them or not, no matter how much money he has
to pay for them. Within a short time, within a few weeks
or even days, the things which were used as money are no
longer used as media of exchange. They become scrap
paper. Nobody wants to give away anything against them."*

—Ludwig von Mises

# Introduction

*I was blind, but now I see.*
*Limitless*

For thousands of years, gold has captivated human civilization. From ancient empires that crowned rulers with it to modern nations that still hold it in reserve, gold has remained a constant across changing monetary systems.

More than a commodity, gold has served as a stabilizing force in times of uncertainty. When currencies weaken and structures strain, gold endures.

This guide prepares you to navigate turbulence. You are living through a moment that demands clear thinking, courage, and personal responsibility. It equips you to face coming hardships with confidence grounded in how monetary systems function.

Institutions fail. Debt becomes unsustainable. Governments overreach. Digital control often expands gradually, making it harder to opt out later. Yet your ability to make independent financial decisions does not vanish. You can build your own foundation and secure your future before instability accelerates. This guide does not attempt to predict collapse. Its purpose is to help you remain prepared and capable, no matter what happens next.

**Inside this guide, you will learn:**

- How global debt, inflation, and institutional fragility are driving the Great Financial Reset, and why gold becomes indispensable during systemic transformation.
- Why the Fourth Turning matters, and how historical cycles explain the societal and economic turbulence we are experiencing today.
- How gold has preserved wealth through centuries of crisis and monetary reset, and why its properties make it the ultimate hedge in times of uncertainty.
- Where gold hides in everyday life, from heirlooms to electronics, and how to recognize opportunities most people overlook.
- How to store gold safely and independently, whether at home or in trusted allocated vaults.

- Why silver complements gold, especially in crisis scenarios where barter, liquidity, and tactical positioning matter.
- How to prepare for future disruptions, including potential currency redenomination, programmable digital currencies, and supply-chain breakdowns.
- How to build generational wealth, preserve family stability, and pass on not just assets, but wisdom.
- Personal stories woven throughout, illustrating hardship, resilience, and the triumph of preparation.

What follows is not theory alone, but a practical framework for navigating uncertain times.

Gold is your anchor.

Gold is your protection.

Gold is your pathway through the storm.

# World Debt and Global Concerns

*Pay no attention to the man behind the curtain.*
*The Wizard of Oz*

We are living through the climax of a grand historical cycle, what *The Fourth Turning* by William Strauss and Neil Howe identifies as the crisis phase. This is the era when institutions deteriorate, frameworks destabilize, and foundational resets occur. The explosive growth of global debt is not merely an economic issue; it is the unmistakable signature of a civilization approaching its inflection point.

## The Modern Economy Built on a Fault Line

Our global financial system resembles a skyscraper built on unstable ground. For decades, governments, corporations, and consumers have accumulated debt far faster than real productivity could support. Much of this debt is mathematically unpayable.

Rather than confront reality, leaders:

- Refinance old debt
- Create new debt
- Expand money supply
- Delay consequences

This creates a world where:

- Debt grows faster than productivity
- Governments rely on constant money creation
- Inflation becomes a hidden tax
- People work harder but feel poorer

Families feel as though they are running faster just to stay in place. Savings shrink. Optimism declines. Economic despair spreads.

## The Ballooning Debt Crisis

Global debt now exceeds hundreds of trillions of dollars, many times global GDP. Debt saturates society. Government debt supports failing programs and geopolitical agendas; corporate debt favors buybacks over innovation, and consumer debt rises across credit cards, student loans, auto loans, and mortgages.

Debt is no longer a tool; it is a dependency.

Governments cannot raise rates without causing defaults. Governments cannot stop printing without collapsing markets. Governments cannot cut spending without destabilizing society. The public feels this fragility instinctively. Trust erodes. Anxiety rises.

## Debt Saturation and the Point of No Return

There is a moment in every debt-based system when borrowing stops solving problems and begins creating them. This moment is rarely announced. It does not arrive with emergency headlines or official declarations. Instead, it arrives quietly when debt grows faster than the economy that must service it.

At that point, debt is no longer leverage. It becomes gravity.

For much of modern history, governments were able to grow their way out of debt. Productivity expanded, populations grew, innovation flourished, and real economic output justified borrowing. That era appears to be ending.

Today, debt grows exponentially while productivity grows linearly, if it grows at all. The arithmetic becomes increasingly unsustainable. Debt-to-GDP ratios rise not because societies are investing productively, but because they are refinancing survival. Old debt is rolled into new debt, then interest is paid with newly created money. Temporary measures become permanent policies. Emergency actions become standard operating procedure.

The debt cycle has reached terminal saturation. Once the debt structure reaches this stage, every decision must serve the debt itself. Interest rates cannot rise without triggering widespread defaults. Spending cannot be reduced without destabilizing society. Money creation cannot stop without collapsing markets. Governments are trapped in a narrow corridor where every exit leads to crisis.

This is not political failure. It is mathematical inevitability.

## Inflation: The Silent Predator

Inflation is the natural consequence of excessive money creation. For everyday people, inflation is not abstract; it is painful. Grocery bills rise, rents and home prices become unaffordable, energy costs climb, and savings erode in real terms. When wages cannot keep up, people feel trapped in a cycle designed to fail them. Inflation destroys more wealth than taxes, yet it is rarely debated honestly.

## Currency Weakness and the Erosion of Purchasing Power

Every major currency has lost enormous purchasing power over the past century because fiat currency can be printed infinitely while gold cannot. As more currency floods the economy, institutions erode, investments grow increasingly risky, and maintaining a standard of living requires greater effort. A growing sense of unease is taking hold, particularly among younger generations who increasingly believe the financial ladder has been pulled away. Fiat currency is increasingly understood as a framework sustained by social agreement rather than intrinsic value.

## The Illusion of Stability

One of the most dangerous features of systemic decline is that it often feels stable until it doesn't. Markets rise. Asset prices inflate. Employment statistics appear healthy. From a distance, the system appears functional. Yet beneath the surface, a quiet divergence takes place: financial markets detach from lived reality.

People work harder yet fall further behind. Savings lose purchasing power. Housing becomes unreachable. Food, energy, healthcare, and education consume an ever-growing share of income. Wealth concentrates upward while risk cascades downward.

This illusion of stability is sustained through debt-fueled stimulus and monetary intervention. Markets are no longer signals of economic health; they are reflections of liquidity injections. Prices rise not because value is increasing, but because currency is weakening.

History shows that collapse does not begin with panic. It begins with confidence. The longer the illusion holds, the sharper the correction becomes.

## Economic Instability and the Emotional Impact

Economic instability does more than disrupt markets; it reshapes identity, confidence, and hope. Stress over savings, fear of job loss, anxiety about retirement, and panic during periods of volatility compound into a growing sense of uncertainty about the future.

A shrinking middle class is not merely an economic problem; it is a psychological crisis.

## Why the Public Always Reacts Too Late

Human psychology is poorly equipped to recognize slow-moving danger. People are wired to respond to visible threats; storms, wars, and fires, not gradual erosion. This is known as normalcy bias: the belief that tomorrow will resemble yesterday simply because it always has.

Trust lingers long after paradigms deserve it. Institutions benefit from inertia. Currency holds value until confidence disappears suddenly. By the time the majority realizes something is wrong, options are limited and exits are crowded. This is how wealth transfers occur, not through dramatic confiscation, but through quiet dilution.

Those who prepare early are not fearful; they are simply aware. History is consistent on this point: those who recognize debt saturation before the crowd preserve wealth. Those who wait for confirmation lose it.

## Government Overreach and the Digital Future

Every Fourth Turning is marked by rising central authority as institutions struggle to maintain control. Today, this manifests through expanding economic oversight and digital tools.

Expanding financial restrictions are already visible in several measurable ways:

- Cash withdrawal limits
- Increased taxation and audits
- Financial surveillance
- Frozen or seized assets during emergencies
- Digital identification programs tied to banking accounts
- Central Bank Digital Currencies (CBDCs)

CBDCs introduce the possibility of programmable money, including oversight over:

- Where you spend
- What you spend on
- When you spend
- How much you can spend

Such decisions may ultimately be dictated by an algorithm. This creates a subtle form of psychological pressure. People want the ability to spend, save, and move wealth without outside permission. Yet they increasingly feel those freedoms slipping away.

## Geopolitical Tension and Fragile Supply Chains

The global economy is interconnected yet inherently fragile. Recent shocks have revealed how easily supply networks fail, from semiconductor shortages and food disruptions to energy crises, shipping gridlock, and geopolitical currency volatility.

People now sense that the continuity they relied upon is more illusion than reality.

## Why Economic Instability Matters So Much

As trust fades in currency, government, and institutions, societies approach the threshold of reset. History shows that such moments coincide with weakening empires, failing currency systems, realigned social structures, and dramatic transfers of wealth.

The Great Financial Reset is the economic expression of the Fourth Turning, a convergence of debt saturation, collapsing trust, technological acceleration, and centralizing power.

People are turning to gold, silver, and self-reliance not out of fear, but out of realization. When debt begins to wobble, instinct drives people toward what cannot be printed, diluted, or redefined.

## Amid the Crisis

This chapter is not intended to create fear, but awareness. Awareness leads to preparation, and preparation allows calmer decisions when structures become unstable. We have seen this pattern before.

Monetary systems stretch beyond sustainability. Debt compounds faster than productivity. Governments intervene more aggressively in an attempt to maintain stability. Confidence erodes quietly before it breaks suddenly. The sequence is not new. It is historical.

Digital governance expands gradually, often presented as convenience or security, until opting out becomes difficult. But your ability to act with foresight does not vanish simply because institutions strain. Preparation is not panic. It is recognition.

This guide does not attempt to predict collapse. Its purpose is simple: to help you remain prepared and capable for whatever comes next.

When trust in financial structures and government institutions declines, especially in periods of overreach, alternative forms of wealth preservation gain importance. Gold serves as a counterbalance to uncertainty, a refuge from surveillance, and a hedge against systems that may not always act in individuals' best interests.

# Why Gold

*This is Sparta!*
*300*

For over 5,000 years, gold has been humanity's chosen symbol of wealth, power, and resilience. Empires have risen and fallen, currencies have come and gone, economic systems have transformed, yet gold remains. It is the only form of money that has survived every war, every crisis, and every transition in human history.

Unlike fiat currency, which is created by political decision, gold emerges from the Earth itself. Its value is not voted on, printed into existence, or digitally manufactured. It is discovered, mined, refined, and earned. As the financial landscape becomes increasingly digital, manipulated, and fragile, gold offers something rare:

Permanence.

## A Universal Wealth Language

Gold is understood everywhere, across cultures, borders, and global economies. A fisherman in Thailand, a banker in London, a farmer in Brazil, and a merchant in India all recognize gold's value instantly.

You don't need translation. You don't need a market. You don't need a government guaranteeing it. Throughout history, gold has served as the world's only truly universal wealth language.

While currencies are border-bound and politically dependent, gold transcends geography. This shared acceptance makes it uniquely powerful during times of upheaval or migration.

## A Hedge Against the Weakening of Paper Money

Every fiat currency in history has eventually lost significant purchasing power.

Not most.

All.

The reasons vary:

- Hyperinflation
- Debasement
- Political collapse
- War
- Overprinting
- Greed

But the result is the same: the currency becomes worthless.

Gold, by contrast, has preserved purchasing power for thousands of years.

Consider these comparisons:

- A Roman soldier's annual pay in gold could buy a high-quality toga, belt, and sandals, roughly equivalent today to a fine suit, belt, and dress shoes.
- One ounce of gold bought a tailored men's outfit in the 1920s; it buys a tailored men's outfit today.
- A home that cost 200–400 ounces of gold a century ago still costs 200–400 ounces today.

Gold protects purchasing power and tends to preserve value across long monetary cycles. Paper money fades. Gold remembers.

## Gold vs. "Safe" Financial Assets

Most people believe they are protected because they own "safe" financial assets. Cash in the bank. Government bonds. Retirement accounts. Broad stock portfolios. These instruments feel secure because they are familiar, regulated, and institutionally endorsed.

But safety depends on context.

Cash is only safe when purchasing power is stable. Bonds are only safe when governments can honor obligations without debasing currency. Equities are only safe when valuations are supported by real productivity rather than monetary expansion. Pensions are only safe when political promises remain solvent.

Gold requires none of these conditions. Gold does not rely on interest rates, fiscal discipline, or institutional credibility. It does not depend on central banks behaving responsibly or governments honoring long-term promises. It is not someone else's liability.

Gold is not a bet on success. It is protection against failure. Gold appears boring when systems are functioning well. Its purpose becomes clear when those systems strain.

## Psychological Safety in an Uncertain World

There is a profound emotional difference between owning physical gold and seeing numbers on a bank screen. Digital balances feel abstract; they can be frozen, altered, or erased. Physical gold feels real because it engages the senses. Its weight conveys strength. Its color suggests permanence. Its coolness in the hand feels grounding. Its indestructibility provides quiet reassurance.

People describe holding gold as calming, almost meditative. It reconnects them with something ancient and true, wealth you can actually touch. When financial systems waver, this psychological foundation becomes priceless.

## Gold and Monetary Resets

Every monetary system in history has eventually reset. The method changes, but the pattern remains consistent.

Resets arrive through:

- Currency redenomination
- Debt restructuring or jubilees
- Capital restrictions
- Banking holidays
- Emergency monetary reforms

In each case, paper claims are altered, diluted, or restricted. What people believed they owned is quietly redefined.

Gold behaves differently. It always has.

Unlike paper assets, gold requires no rescue. It requires no policy intervention. Its value does not depend on confidence being restored. Currency resets do not destroy gold; they reprice it. What once required hundreds of currency units now requires thousands.

Not because gold changed, but because the measuring stick broke. This is why gold must be accumulated *before* a reset occurs. Once trust collapses, access disappears. Premiums explode. Supply tightens. Governments intervene.

Gold is the constant when money resets.

## Gold as the Anti-Debt Asset

Modern money is built on debt. Gold rests on intrinsic value. Every time governments print money, they create debt. Money comes into existence only because something is owed.

In contrast, gold stands apart. It is not anyone's liability, not backed by a government promise, not tied to a bank's balance sheet, and it cannot go bankrupt. Gold requires no trust. This independence makes gold the cornerstone of direct financial control.

## Crisis-Proof Wealth

During every major crisis in history, gold served as the ultimate insurance policy.

- **Wars?**

Gold allowed families to relocate, barter, or buy safety when currencies collapsed.

- **Hyperinflation?**

In Weimar Germany, gold saved entire households that would have otherwise lost everything to inflation.

- **Financial Crises?**

During the 2008 crash, gold rose while markets collapsed.

- **Bank Failures?**

When banks freeze withdrawals, gold remains fully accessible.

No matter the disaster: economic, political, or natural, gold is one of the few assets that consistently retains value. People instinctively turn to it when everything else begins to break.

## Independence From Government Control

The rise of digital currencies and expanding surveillance makes gold more important than ever. Governments can freeze accounts, limit withdrawals, tax aggressively, monitor spending, implement digital identification protocols, and roll out programmable currencies, expanding control over financial activity.

But they cannot track, freeze, or manipulate physical gold you hold privately.

Physical gold exists outside the system. It cannot be censored. It represents freedom in tangible form.

## Why Central Banks Never Truly Abandon Gold

Despite public narratives suggesting gold is a relic, central banks have never abandoned it. In fact, they continue to accumulate gold quietly and strategically.

Gold occupies the highest tier of reserve assets because it carries zero counterparty risk. It is the only monetary asset that does not depend on another entity's promise to retain value.

Central banks understand something the public is rarely told: gold is not obsolete; it remains foundational.

When trust between nations weakens, gold settles accounts. When currencies compete, gold neutralizes politics. When systems fracture, gold restores balance.

Individuals who hold gold are not resisting the prevailing order. They are mirroring its deepest instincts without leverage, opacity, or political exposure. Gold is not outside the financial architecture by accident. It is outside by design.

## Gold and Time: The Ultimate Relationship

Gold is one of the few assets that becomes more valuable as instability increases. Over long periods, it outlasts economic cycles, recessions, depressions, political turmoil, currency resets, and even technological disruptions.

Gold does not rust, tarnish, or decay. Gold does not rely on electricity, servers, or institutions. Gold does not expire or degrade. Every ounce of gold ever mined still exists. The longer the timeline, the more gold proves itself.

## The Moral of Gold

Gold does not promise quick riches. It offers resilience, security, and greater control over your financial future. It encourages long-term thinking in a world obsessed with instant gratification. It rewards discipline, protects families, and bridges generations.

Gold is more than a metal. It embodies security, patience, responsibility, and freedom. It reflects a philosophy of endurance. It does what modern structures often fail to do: it tells the truth. Historically, gold reveals the true state of the economy. It exposes currency weakness, reflects global uncertainty, and responds to trust and distrust in governments and institutions.

When people sense danger, they buy gold. When structures weaken, gold strengthens. When currencies fail, gold prevails.

Always.

Gold is more than a hedge. It is a foundation you can build your life upon.

Even as the world shifts toward a tightly monitored digital financial architecture, even as debt spirals, inflation rises, and trust fades, you hold something real, timeless, and powerful. You hold history. You hold security. You hold hope made metal. Gold reminds you that even if the world becomes unstable, your future does not have to.

# Properties of Gold

*There is no spoon.*
*The Matrix*

Gold is more than a precious metal; it is a chemical miracle, a cultural icon, a practical tool, and a timeless store of value. Understanding its physical properties and various forms deepens your appreciation for why gold, among all metals on Earth, became humanity's ultimate benchmark of wealth.

## A Metal Born From Stars

Gold did not originate on Earth. It formed during violent supernova explosions or the collision of neutron stars billions of years ago. These cosmic events forged heavy elements, including gold, and scattered them throughout the universe.

Every ounce of gold you hold is literally extraterrestrial.

## Gold's Atomic Identity

- Atomic Number: 79
- Symbol: Au (from the Latin aurum, meaning "shining dawn")
- Atomic Weight: 196.967
- Electron Configuration: A uniquely stable structure that gives gold its famous yellow luster and resistance to tarnish.

Gold's atomic structure makes it nearly chemically immortal.

## Why Gold and Not Other Metals

Many materials on Earth are valuable. Very few are monetary.

Silver is useful and historically important, but it is bulky and volatile. Platinum is rarer than gold, yet heavily dependent on industrial demand. Copper is essential to civilization but far too abundant to function as money. Digital assets rely on electricity, networks, and enforcement mechanisms that must remain intact for value to exist.

Gold occupies a narrow and extraordinary position between these extremes. It is rare enough to hold value, yet abundant enough to be divisible and usable. It is chemically inert, meaning it does not corrode, decay, or degrade. It is easily recognizable, difficult to counterfeit convincingly, and universally accepted without explanation.

Gold does not compete with technology or industry. It exists above them as a measure of value rather than a tool of production. This is why civilizations that never interacted, never communicated, and never shared culture all arrived at the same conclusion:

Gold was chosen, not imposed.

## Why Gold Is Unique in the Natural World

Gold's unique role as money is not accidental. Its physical and chemical properties make it well suited to function as a durable store of value.

### 1. It Does Not Tarnish

Unlike most metals, gold doesn't rust, oxidize, or degrade. This is why ancient gold artifacts look almost unchanged after thousands of years.

### 2. It Is Exceptionally Malleable

Gold is the most malleable metal known, meaning it can be shaped and stretched without breaking:

- One ounce can be hammered into a sheet covering 100 square feet.
- A single gram can be drawn into a wire 2 kilometers long.

This remarkable flexibility made gold invaluable for jewelry, art, and intricate currency designs.

## 3. It Conducts Heat and Electricity Efficiently

Gold is an excellent conductor of both heat and electricity, making it highly valuable in advanced technology where reliability is critical.

Gold is used in:

- Smartphones
- Computers
- Medical devices
- Satellites
- Spacecraft

Its resistance to corrosion ensures long-term reliability, which is why gold remains essential in high-performance electronics.

## 4. It Is Dense and Heavy

Gold's density (19.32 g/cm$^3$) gives it an unmistakable weight in the hand, one reason why counterfeits are easy to detect by experienced investors.

Even small pieces feel substantial, reinforcing gold's reputation as tangible and trustworthy wealth.

## 5. It Is Rare, but Not Too Rare

If gold were too abundant, it wouldn't be valuable. If it were too scarce, it wouldn't be practical as money.

Nature gave humanity the perfect balance. This rare equilibrium is one reason gold continues to serve as a dependable store of value across generations.

## Scarcity Beyond Rarity

True scarcity is not simply about how little of something exists. It is about how slowly new supply can be created.

Gold's supply grows at approximately 1–2 percent per year. This growth rate has remained remarkably stable over centuries, regardless of price, demand, or technology. Even when gold prices rise sharply, production cannot be significantly accelerated.

This constraint is crucial. Digital scarcity can be created instantly. New currencies, tokens, or financial instruments can appear overnight. Gold cannot be conjured into existence. Every ounce requires exploration, energy, labor, time, and risk. This embedded cost anchors gold's value in physical reality. Gold's supply expands at a pace that mirrors long-term population growth and economic expansion. It neither overwhelms the system with abundance nor strangles it through scarcity.

This balance is not accidental. It is why gold has functioned as money for thousands of years.

## Purity Levels and What They Mean

Gold is alloyed with other metals for hardness, durability, or color variation.

### Common Purities:

| Purity | Karat | Fineness Mark | Typical Use |
|---|---|---|---|
| 99.99% | 24k | 9999 | Investment bars, bullion coins |
| 99.9% | 24k | 999 | Most gold bars, coins |
| 91.7% | 22k | 917 | Jewelry, sovereign coins |
| 75% | 18k | 750 | High-end jewelry |
| 58.5% | 14k | 585 | Standard jewelry |
| 41.7% | 10k | 417 | Durable jewelry |

## Hallmarks You May See:

- 999 or 999.9 — Pure bullion
- Au 750 — 18k gold
- Au 585 — 14k gold
- 916/917 — 22k gold

## Understanding Gold Colors

Gold naturally appears yellow, but alloys create variations:

- Yellow Gold: Traditional alloy with silver and copper
- Rose Gold: Copper-heavy alloy giving a reddish hue
- White Gold: Alloyed with palladium, nickel, or platinum
- Green Gold: Mixed with silver
- Black Gold: Surface-treated or alloyed with cobalt

These are primarily used in jewelry, not investment bullion.

## Forms of Gold: Choosing What's Right for You

Seasoned bullion investors prioritize weight, purity, and premium over decorative design. The forms listed below offer advantages depending on liquidity, storage, and intended use.

### 1. Gold Coins

Gold coins are highly recognizable, easy to sell, and often government-backed. Their standardized weight and purity make them easy for buyers and dealers to verify quickly.

Examples include:

- American Gold Eagle
- American Gold Buffalo

- Pre-1933 U.S. Gold Coins (Historic)
- Canadian Maple Leaf
- South African Krugerrand
- British Britannia
- Austrian Philharmonic

Coins are ideal for liquidity and widespread acceptance. In many markets, these coins command strong trust and can be sold almost anywhere in the world.

## 2. Gold Bars

Gold bars are the most direct and efficient way to hold physical gold in larger quantities.

Bars come in many sizes:

- 1 gram
- 5 grams
- 10 grams
- 1 ounce (31.1 g)
- 50 grams
- 100 grams
- 1 kilogram (32.15 oz)
- 400-ounce Good Delivery bars (the standard used by central banks and major bullion markets)

Most recognizable gold bars:

- PAMP Suisse (Lady Fortuna)
- Credit Suisse
- Perth Mint

Bars typically carry lower premiums and are efficient for high-value storage. For investors focused on accumulating weight rather than collectability, gold bars often provide the most cost-effective way to build substantial holdings.

## 3. Gold Rounds

Gold rounds are privately minted and do not carry government backing. They are efficient for stacking and often serve as lower-cost alternatives to bullion coins. Gold rounds are available in a wide range of sizes, styles, and designs, with the one-ounce round being the most common.

Most recognizable gold rounds include:

- Buffalo Gold Round
- Saint-Gaudens Replica Round
- Morgan Design Round
- Walking Liberty Round
- Sunshine Mint Round

## 4. Jewelry (Wearable Wealth)

Gold jewelry has served as a form of personal savings for centuries, combining beauty, cultural meaning, and financial value.

**Pros:**

- Cultural significance
- Utility during emergencies
- Cross-border portability

**Cons:**

- Higher premiums
- Variable purity

Jewelry can serve as portable savings, especially in countries where banks are distrusted.

## 5. Scrap Gold

Scrap gold refers to broken, outdated, or unwanted gold items that still retain their intrinsic metal value.

Scrap gold is found in:

- Old forgotten jewelry boxes
- Dental gold
- Electronics
- Old watches and pens
- Estate sales
- Online marketplaces (junk, scrap, broken)

Often refined and recycled, scrap gold can offer a low-cost entry point for savvy buyers.

## Investment-Grade vs Consumer Gold

Not all gold is acquired for the same purpose. Understanding the distinction between investment-grade and consumer gold helps investors choose the form that best matches their goals.

### Investment-Grade Gold

- Purity: 99.9% or higher
- Certified by mints
- Comes with assay cards or serial numbers
- Ideal for long-term storage and wealth preservation

### Consumer-Grade Gold

- Jewelry and collectibles
- Purity varies
- Requires testing (acid test, electronic, XRF)

Understanding this distinction helps you choose the right form of gold for your strategy, whether your priority is long-term preservation, everyday liquidity, or practical ownership.

## Why Gold Resists Confiscation

Throughout history, governments have attempted to control or confiscate gold. These efforts have met with limited success, not because gold is invincible, but because its nature resists centralized authority.

Gold is portable; large amounts of value can be carried discreetly. Gold is fungible. One ounce is interchangeable with another. Gold is durable. It can be hidden, buried, passed down, or worn without loss of value.

Unlike digital assets or registered accounts, gold does not require ongoing permission to exist. This decentralization makes large-scale confiscation difficult to enforce and easy to evade. While laws can be written, compliance is another matter entirely.

Gold survives not because it defies authority, but because it operates outside dependency. This is why gold has endured through empires, revolutions, reforms, and resets.

## How to Verify Authenticity

Authenticity is critical when acquiring physical gold. While counterfeit gold is relatively uncommon in reputable markets, verifying authenticity protects both your capital and your confidence. Gold is often counterfeited using tungsten, which has a similar density.

True experts rely on multiple tests:

- Weight and dimensions
- Magnet test (gold is non-magnetic)
- Ping test (distinct sound)
- Density test
- XRF (professional grading)
- Ultrasound scanning

For significant purchases, always buy from reputable dealers or recognized mints. Request assay certificates or independent verification to confirm the metal's purity and authenticity.

## The Emotional Impact of Holding Physical Gold

Beyond science and economics, holding gold evokes a deep psychological reaction. It connects you to ancient civilizations, generations of savers, human history, and the survival instincts that drive people to protect what they own.

Gold in the hand feels like truth: heavy, incorruptible, eternal. That emotional connection is why gold remains the cornerstone of financial preparedness.

## Why Understanding Gold's Physical Nature Matters

When you understand why gold behaves the way it does, you begin to see:

- Why it resists manipulation
- Why it survives every crisis
- Why it became money
- Why governments hold it
- Why central banks buy it

Gold is not valuable because governments say so. Governments are valuable because they hold gold.

Gold is more than a metal. It is integrity in physical form. When you hold gold, you hold history and the strength to navigate what comes next.

As monetary structures drift toward digital fragility and centralized authority, gold remains a physical anchor, a reminder that some truths never change.

# Treasure Hunt

*I am everywhere.*
*Lucy*

Gold isn't just in vaults, coins, and jewelry shops. It hides in plain sight, in heirlooms, forgotten drawers, thrift stores, discarded electronics, old estates, and even the memories of your family. Most people walk past gold every day without realizing it.

## The Mindset of a Gold Finder

Before diving into locations, you must cultivate the right mindset:

### ✓ Be Curious

Gold reveals itself to people who ask questions, inspect details, and look where others don't.

### ✓ Be Patient

Gold finding rewards slow, thoughtful effort, not rushing.

### ✓ Be Observant

Small hallmarks, subtle color differences, and weight clues separate treasure from junk.

### ✓ Be Respectful and Ethical

Many gold-finding opportunities involve people's sentimental items or estates. Integrity ensures good deals and lifelong relationships.

Your most important tool isn't a neodymium rare earth magnet, a loupe, or a scale. It's your awareness.

*Eyes open, no fear.*

## Gold as a Skill, Not Just an Asset

Gold ownership is powerful. Gold literacy is transformative.

Most people believe wealth is something you buy. In reality, wealth is something you learn to recognize. The ability to identify gold by weight, color, markings, density, and feel is a skill that compounds over time and survives conditions where money alone does not.

Skills remain when systems fail. Capital does not always follow.

Those who understand gold are not dependent on perfect markets or honest pricing. They can evaluate value in imperfect conditions: estate clear-outs, mislabeled items, emotional sales, neglected collections. This ability creates opportunity regardless of economic climate. Success often comes from learning to recognize overlooked value.

Once acquired, this skill becomes permanent. Inflation cannot erode it. Policy cannot confiscate it. Digital systems cannot disable it. As judgment is increasingly outsourced, the ability to recognize value becomes a form of independent agency.

## 1. Jewelry: The Most Abundant Everyday Source

Most gold in daily life comes from jewelry, yet much of it goes unnoticed or undervalued.

Places where gold jewelry appears unexpectedly:

- Estate sales
- Yard sales
- Thrift stores
- Flea markets

- Jewelry boxes of older relatives
- Pawnshops with poorly labeled items
- Abandoned storage units
- Auction lots sold "as-is"

Signs you've found real gold:

- Hallmarks: 10k, 14k, 18k, 22k, 24k; 375, 585, 750, 916, 999
- The magnet test (real gold is non-magnetic)
- Weight: gold is heavier than it looks
- Smooth edges and quality craftsmanship
- No peeling or flaking on "yellow gold"

Why jewelry is powerful wealth:

- Portable
- Recognizable worldwide
- Easy to barter
- Emotionally meaningful
- Useful in emergencies

In many countries, wearable gold functions as a form of private banking. It can be that for you as well.

## 2. Electronics: The Hidden Gold Mine in Technology

Modern devices contain small but valuable traces of gold. Though each piece is tiny, the quantity adds up when you collect at scale.

Devices containing gold:

- Older computers and circuit boards
- Phones (especially early smartphones)
- Laptops
- Radios
- Cameras
- Gaming consoles
- Industrial connectors

Why Gold?

Gold is used because it never corrodes and electronics require reliable conductivity.

High-yield items include:

- 1980s and 1990s circuit boards
- Server boards
- Vintage telecommunications equipment
- Gold-plated connectors and pins
- RAM modules from early PCs

Gold recovery requires chemical processes, but many people profit simply by selling scrap electronics to refiners.

This is a modern form of urban mining and a practical skill in a world overflowing with discarded tech.

## 3. Thrift Stores, Pawnshops & Antique Markets

Opportunities to find overlooked gold appear in places most people ignore:

### Thrift Stores

Employees are rarely trained to identify precious metals, and jewelry is often sorted quickly with minimal evaluation. As a result, genuine gold pieces may be mistakenly grouped with costume jewelry or priced based on appearance rather than metal content.

You may occasionally find:

- 14k or 18k gold rings priced for a few dollars
- Gold chains mixed into bulk "grab bags" of assorted jewelry
- Sterling silver pieces containing small gold components
- Vintage watches that contain gold cases or gold-filled parts

## Pawnshops

Many pawnshop owners focus primarily on issuing short-term loans rather than evaluating the intrinsic metal value of jewelry. As a result, mid-tier gold pieces such as chains, rings, and small scrap items are sometimes priced quickly based on weight estimates or resale assumptions. This can create opportunities for knowledgeable buyers who recognize the true gold content and current melt value.

## Antique Markets

Older dealers often price jewelry and decorative items based on craftsmanship, design appeal, or perceived age rather than the underlying metal value. When gold pieces lack gemstones or obvious historical significance, they may be overlooked or discounted. Buyers who understand hallmarks, purity marks, and melt value can occasionally acquire genuine gold items well below their intrinsic worth.

Opportunities appear wherever knowledge is unevenly distributed.

## 4. Family Heirlooms and Inherited Items

Most families own more gold than they realize.

You might find gold in:

- Old dormant jewelry boxes
- Unworn wedding bands
- Religious items
- Vintage lighters
- Lockets and chains
- Pocket watches
- Old pens
- Eyewear
- Coins received decades ago

Gold is not rare in daily life. It is rare in awareness.

Most overlooked gold exists because of behavioral inefficiencies rather than physical scarcity. Inherited items are frequently undervalued because emotional distance replaces curiosity. Estates prioritize speed over precision. Sellers want closure, not optimization. Buyers lack training.

Modern society also disconnects people from physical money. Digital balances feel "real" because they are visible. Physical assets feel "old" because they require attention. As a result, gold passes hands at a fraction of its worth, not because it lacks value, but because value is no longer widely understood.

This is not a temporary condition. It is structural. Often, people forget the value of items passed down through generations. Gold carries memories, but it also carries weight in hard times. Understanding its value helps preserve financial wealth and family legacy.

As long as knowledge remains unevenly distributed, opportunity persists.

## 5. Scrap, Recycling & "Unloved Gold"

Gold is frequently found in damaged or broken pieces:

- Bent rings
- Single earrings
- Broken chains
- Tangled piles of jewelry
- Old dental gold
- Plaques and medals

To most people, these pieces are trash. To someone who understands gold, they are wealth. Knowing how to test, weigh, and evaluate gold makes you a smart buyer and a valuable resource to others who want to sell unwanted items.

## 6. Gold Coins: Hidden Wealth in Plain Sight

People often inherit or discover coins without fully understanding their value.

Common accidental finds include:

- U.S. Gold Eagles
- Krugerrands
- Canadian Maples
- Sovereigns
- Pre-1933 U.S. gold coins

These coins may sit untouched in drawers, safes, or old collections for decades.

Gold coins offer several advantages:

- High purity
- Easy authentication
- Global recognition
- Quick liquidity

Finding even one can feel like discovering a time capsule of wealth.

## 7. Places Most People Overlook

A skilled gold hunter knows to search where others don't bother looking.

Undervalued areas include:

- Abandoned storage units
- Architectural salvage
- Auction house "mixed lots"
- Vintage toolboxes (containing gold-plated parts)
- Old military gear
- Broken watches
- Dentists retiring or selling equipment
- Flea markets offering "junk jewelry" by the bag
- Thrift store jewelry racks

Gold hides in the ordinary.

## 8. Gold Verification: Learning to Reject Fakes

To find gold with confidence, you must first learn to reject fakes.

Quick tests include:

- Non-magnetic
- Proper weight
- Hallmarks
- Nitric acid test
- Electronic gold tester
- XRF scanner (high-end)
- The "ping test" for coins or scratch test for jewelry

Knowing how to detect real gold elevates you from casual seeker to knowledgeable collector.

## From Finder to Steward

The purpose of finding gold is not consumption. It is consolidation. A finder looks for opportunity. A steward protects outcome.

Stewardship means knowing when to sell and when to hold. It means converting small wins into lasting reserves. It means resisting the urge to trade real value for temporary comfort.

Gold found cheaply becomes gold held permanently.

This transition from finder to steward marks a shift from curiosity to responsibility and from short-term gain to lasting control. Those who steward gold think in decades, not transactions. They understand that each piece recovered, identified, or preserved strengthens resilience and reduces reliance on fragile systems.

Gold rewards patience. Stewardship multiplies it.

## Why Finding Gold Matters More Today Than Ever

As inflation rises and digital networks dominate, privacy erodes and purchasing power declines.

Gold in daily life becomes a powerful survival skill. Finding gold is not scavenging; it is reclaiming forgotten wealth in a world losing touch with real value. Gold finding provides financial opportunity, practical skills, and the ability to rely less on unstable frameworks. It teaches you to see beneath the surface of everyday objects and understand that wealth is often hidden where others fail to look.

Gold surrounds you, not in vaults or bank accounts, but in the overlooked corners of modern life. Each discovery, whether a simple ring or a high-grade circuit board, represents a moment of empowerment.

When you learn to find gold, you learn to recognize value in a world obsessed with illusions. And in doing so, you become the type of person who not only sees opportunity but creates it.

# Be Your Own Bank

*Never tell anyone outside the family what you're thinking.*
*The Godfather*

## "The Basement Safe"

The basement always smelled like old newspapers and cedarwood, the kind of place where forgotten things waited patiently to be remembered. I wasn't supposed to explore down there alone, but curiosity won that day. While digging behind a stack of dusty boxes, my flashlight beam landed on something unexpected: a small iron safe, rusted but proud, like a treasure chest from a pirate story I used to imagine.

With a few determined tugs, I pulled it into the open. It wasn't locked.

Inside were three gold coins wrapped in a faded handkerchief and a folded slip of paper. The handwriting was shaky but confident:

*"Real security is what you hold in your hands, not what a bank promises on paper."*

I didn't understand the message then, but later, my grandmother explained that those coins had helped our family through difficult times: layoffs, inflation spikes, and the kind of crises people rarely talk about but always remember.

She told me something I never forgot:

*"Money can vanish. Wealth stays with those who prepare."*

That moment planted a seed in me. Not fear, but responsibility. A quiet belief that I could protect my own future, no matter how chaotic the world might become. It was the first time I realized something life-changing:

*"I don't need permission to be secure. I just need wisdom."*

## Why Banking Became Fragile

Modern banking was never designed for resilience. It was designed for efficiency, leverage, and expansion. Over time, safety was replaced by speed, and stability by scale. What once functioned as a custodial service gradually transformed into a complex web of lending, rehypothecation, and derivative exposure.

Banks no longer store wealth. They circulate promises.

Under fractional-reserve systems, deposits are lent, layered, and reused across balance sheets. This structure works only as long as confidence remains intact. Once trust falters, liquidity vanishes. Withdrawals are limited. Access becomes conditional. Emergency rules replace normal rights.

History shows this pattern repeatedly, not because banks are malicious, but because the structure itself is fragile.

Gold sits outside this fragility. To be your own bank is not to reject modern finance entirely. It is to remove blind dependence on it. Being your own bank does not mean storing every ounce yourself. It means retaining control over where, how, and under whose terms your wealth is held.

Owning physical gold is more than a financial decision; it is a declaration of independence. Holding gold makes you your own vault, your own central bank, and your own guarantor of safety. You step outside the vulnerable digital networks and regain direct command over a portion of your wealth. But with that power comes responsibility: once accumulated, how you store your gold determines how effective it will be when you need it most. This chapter dives deeply into home storage, private vaults, international diversification, and the world's most reputable firms for segregated, allocated storage: arrangements where you retain 100% ownership of specific bars or coins.

## The Philosophy of Self-Banking

Most people panic when banks freeze withdrawals or when markets collapse. But those who keep a portion of their wealth in tangible form outside traditional banking experience something priceless:

Calm.

Gold allows you to sleep at night knowing:

- Your wealth cannot be deleted
- Your assets cannot be frozen
- Your purchasing power cannot be inflated away
- Your savings do not depend on political mistakes
- Your money does not need permission to be used

This is what it means to truly own your wealth.

## Self-Custody vs. Delegated Control

Delegated control feels convenient. Someone else safeguards assets, manages records, and grants access. But delegation introduces vulnerability: rules can change, access can be denied, and ownership can be redefined during emergencies. Convenience often masks the quiet transfer of control from the individual to the institution.

Self-custody reverses this equation.

When you hold gold directly, whether personally or through fully allocated, segregated storage, you eliminate counterparty risk. No balance sheet sits between you and your wealth. No algorithm approves your access. No institution interprets your rights. Your wealth exists independently of institutional stability or digital permission.

Self-banking restores a fundamental truth: ownership means possession, not permission.

## 1. Home Storage: Building a Private Fortress

Storing part of your gold at home gives immediate access during emergencies. However, it must be done intelligently, discreetly, and securely.

**Home Storage Principles:**

### ✓ Silence Is the First Rule

No neighbors. No extended family. No online bragging. Your security depends on others not knowing you have gold.

### ✓ Use Multiple Hiding Locations

Diversification works inside the home too. Never keep all gold in one place.

### ✓ Invest in a Real Safe

Look for:

- TL-15 or TL-30 ratings
- Fire and water resistance
- Bolt-down capability
- Concealed placement

### ✓ Consider Decoy Safes

A cheap "discoverable safe" with small valuables inside can prevent burglars from continuing to search.

## 2. Private Vaulting: The Gold Standard of Security

Private vaulting is fundamentally different from bank safe deposit boxes.

Why private vaults are superior to banks:

- Accessible even during banking crises
- Outside the traditional financial system
- Highly insured
- Professionally secured
- No reporting of your holdings (depending on jurisdiction)
- No exposure to banking failures or government freezes

Most importantly:

Private vaults can offer fully segregated and 100% allocated storage.

This means you own specific bars and coins. Your items are held in isolation, not pooled. Bars carry serial numbers tying them to you. The vault cannot legally rehypothecate or lend your metals. You are protected if the facility ever closes or changes ownership.

This is the highest standard of precious metal storage in the world.

## 3. International Diversification: Geography is Protection

To protect against government overreach, currency controls, or extreme political events, many investors spread their precious metals across multiple countries. Ideal jurisdictions offer strong private property rights, low corruption, strict privacy laws, no capital restrictions, and political neutrality.

Serious precious metals investors often store a portion of their holdings in professional private vaults located in politically stable jurisdictions. Allocated or segregated storage ensures the metals are held in the investor's name, fully insured, and independently audited. Diversifying storage across multiple jurisdictions strengthens protection against political risk, financial instability, and access restrictions.

Examples include:

- Switzerland
- Singapore
- Cayman Islands
- Ireland (through GoldCore)

Global diversification means no single authority holds power over all your wealth.

## 4. Top-Tier Firms for Segregated & Allocated Storage

These companies are known for transparency, direct physical ownership, segregated storage standards, and world-class security. The following profiles highlight the strengths of each firm:

### GoldCore (Ireland, UK, Switzerland)

GoldCore is a well-established precious metals firm offering secure storage and ownership solutions for investors seeking international diversification. It is widely regarded as one of Europe's most trusted precious metals firms.

### They Specialize In:

- Segregated, allocated storage
- Offshore storage in Switzerland, Singapore, London, and Ireland
- No pooled accounts
- Direct legal ownership of your gold
- Ability to take physical delivery anytime

They are known for excellent customer service and regulatory compliance.

### BFI Bullion (Switzerland)

BFI, based in Switzerland, operates in one of the strongest jurisdictions for true private banking and secure asset storage.

### What Makes Them Elite:

- 100% allocated gold
- Ultra-secure Swiss vaults
- No exposure to the banking system
- Institutional-grade metal handling
- Multi-signature custody
- Long-term generational wealth services

BFI is designed for clients who value privacy, neutrality, and absolute asset protection.

## GoldBroker.com (France, Switzerland, Canada)

GoldBroker specializes in owner-direct precious metals storage, allowing investors to hold physical gold outside the traditional banking system with direct ownership and no intermediaries.

## Key Advantages:

- You own gold directly in your name
- Vaults located in Switzerland and Canada
- Full segregation (no pooled metal)
- No counterparty risk
- Direct audit access; you can inspect your gold
- Ability to choose bar sizes & mints

Their emphasis on owner-direct storage eliminates third-party risk.

## SWP Cayman (Strategic Wealth Preservation)

SWP Cayman operates one of the world's most modern and geopolitically secure vaults. It is located in the Cayman Islands, a tax-neutral and politically stable jurisdiction outside U.S. and EU oversight.

## Why SWP Is Exceptional:

- Private, non-bank vault
- 100% allocated & segregated storage
- Access to your metals 6 days a week
- U.S.-friendly but offshore
- Zero reporting to governments
- Strong insurance and auditing standards
- Ideal for diversification outside North America

Many investors choose SWP because it offers both convenience and offshore protection.

## The Reason You Store Gold: It Becomes Your Bank

Storing physical gold changes your relationship with money in several ways:

✓ You hold real wealth; no permission needed

✓ There is no middleman, no banker, no gatekeeper

✓ Gold cannot be digitally shut off or frozen

✓ You can relocate or use it anywhere in the world

✓ Your purchasing power remains intact

✓ You own wealth that governments cannot inflate away

When people remove a portion of their wealth from unstable financial environments something unexpected happens. Fear and anxiety fade. Reaction gives way to planning. Decision-making slows and improves.

Gold does not promise riches. It promises continuity.

This psychological shift is one of the most overlooked benefits of self-banking. It restores the ability to make financial decisions without waiting for permission from institutions.

Gold doesn't make you wealthy overnight. It makes you unshakeable over time.

## The Psychology of Safe Storage

Secure storage is not only a logistical decision; it is a psychological one. Knowing that your wealth is protected and directly under your control changes how you think, plan, and respond during periods of volatility.

People who store gold intelligently experience:

- Reduced anxiety
- Quiet confidence
- Calm during crisis
- Relief from economic uncertainty
- Peace of mind from holding real money

The result is deliberate decision-making when others are under pressure. The psychological effect of real ownership is often underestimated.

Storing gold is not about fear; it is about wisdom. It is about building a foundation that no crisis, no inflation, no policy error, and no digital control mechanism can shake.

When you store gold securely, whether at home or in world-class vaults such as GoldCore, BFI Bullion, GoldBroker, or SWP Cayman, you create a layer of protection around your wealth that few assets can match. As economic uncertainty accelerates, that protection becomes increasingly valuable.

# Gold vs Silver

*If you can't spot the sucker in the first half hour, you are the sucker.*
*Rounders*

Gold and silver have served as humanity's twin monetary metals for thousands of years. They are the oldest forms of real money, outlasting every empire, financial system, and political ideology. Both preserve wealth, but they serve different roles, much like a shield and a sword.

Understanding the distinctions between gold and silver gives you more than financial knowledge; it gives you tactical choices in a world where paper wealth is rapidly decaying.

## The Shared Heritage of Gold and Silver

Gold and silver have served humanity as money for thousands of years, forming the foundation of trade, savings, and economic exchange across civilizations. While their roles differed, together they created a monetary partnership that balanced everyday commerce with long-term wealth preservation.

For over 5,000 years:

- Gold was the wealth of kings, empires, and long-term savings.
- Silver was the money of merchants, farmers, and everyday transactions.

Together, these metals tell a story of human civilization: one of scarcity, trust, survival, and recurring economic cycles.

## Two Metals, Two Functions

Gold and silver are often spoken of together, but they serve different roles.

Understanding this distinction transforms how they should be used.

Gold concentrates value. Silver distributes it.

Gold excels at storing large purchasing power discreetly. Silver excels at enabling everyday exchange. One preserves long-term strategic stewardship of wealth. The other supports daily survival.

If gold is strategic wealth, silver is tactical money. Confusing these roles leads to misuse: spending gold too early or overburdening silver with long-term storage. Used together, they form a complete and resilient monetary system.

## Why Gold Leads: The Wealth Anchor

Gold is humanity's universal store of value.

People gravitate to gold because:

- It is compact, high value in a small weight
- It is stable, low volatility compared to silver
- It is globally recognized and trusted
- It is held by central banks as a core reserve asset
- It is unmatched in wealth preservation over centuries

Gold behaves like the quiet guardian of wealth: steady, reliable, and unshakable.

## Why Silver Matters: The People's Money

While gold concentrates wealth, silver has traditionally served as the metal of everyday exchange.

Silver offers several distinct advantages:

- More affordable
- Tied to industrial demand

- Moves more violently in bull markets
- Provides greater percentage gains
- Ideal for barter and small transactions

Silver carries a different energy: more reactive, more dynamic, more emotional. Where gold whispers, silver shouts.

## The Gold-to-Silver Ratio: History's Value Meter

The gold-to-silver ratio is one of the most powerful strategic tools in the precious metals market.

Historically:

- The ratio was ~12:1 to 16:1 for centuries (based on natural mining ratios).

In the modern era:

- 60:1 – 100:1 or higher: common during severe financial distress
- 30:1: excellent
- 20:1: exceptional
- 15:1: rare opportunity
- 10:1 and below: historic crisis level

A high ratio signals:

- Silver may be underpriced
- A future silver surge is likely

A low ratio signals:

- Silver is strong
- Gold may be the better buy

Smart investors "ride the ratio," swapping metals over time rather than spending new money. This strategy builds wealth quietly and efficiently.

## Volatility Is Not Risk, Misuse Is

Silver's volatility often intimidates newcomers. Yet volatility itself is not risk. Misunderstanding volatility is.

Silver's price reflects its dual nature as both a monetary metal and an industrial input. During periods of monetary stress, silver often lags gold at first, then accelerates sharply as affordability drives demand.

This behavior creates opportunity, but only for those prepared for movement.

Gold stabilizes wealth. Silver amplifies it. Used correctly, volatility becomes leverage rather than danger.

## "The First Swap"

I was barely getting by. Rent, bills, and a thin paycheck created the typical early-adult balancing act. Even so, something in me insisted on buying gold, even if I could only afford a little.

I walked into a coin shop with a few crumpled bills in my pocket, expecting to leave empty-handed.

The owner, an older man with silver hair and kind eyes, listened patiently as I asked about gold. Then he smiled and shook his head.

*"You don't need to start with gold,"* he said. *"Let me show you something."*

He placed a few silver Buffalo rounds on the counter, bright, heavy, honest.

Then he explained the gold-to-silver ratio, how silver was the working person's gateway into real, tangible assets. I traded my small savings for a modest stack of silver.

Walking out of the shop that day, I didn't feel broke. I felt energized.

Those silver rounds stayed with me for years, through moves, breakups, job losses, and moments when I felt like I was starting from zero. They never left my side.

And every time I held them, I remembered:

You may start small, but starting is everything.

That small act of calm confidence carried me further than any paycheck ever could.

## Gresham's Law in Action: The Disappearing Metals

Throughout history, from Rome to Weimar Germany to modern Argentina, whenever governments debased currencies, silver coins vanished first, followed by gold.

Today, as fiat collapses slowly across the world, investors are doing exactly what Gresham's Law predicts:

They are pulling real money, gold and silver, out of conventional finance and into private hands.

Gresham's Law famously states:

*"Bad money drives out good money."*

This law helps explain why:

- Gold and silver disappear from circulation
- Fiat currency becomes dominant during inflation
- People hoard "good money" and spend only the weaker currency

## Historical Ratios and Strategic Swaps

The gold-to-silver ratio is more than a statistic. It is a historical signal reflecting relative scarcity, confidence, and monetary stress. Extreme ratio levels signal imbalance, not certainty, but opportunity.

Strategic investors respond by exchanging ounces rather than spending new currency. This approach requires patience, discipline, and emotional detachment. It rewards those who think in cycles rather than headlines.

Over time, quiet swaps compound wealth without increasing exposure.

**Volatility: The Double-Edged Sword of Silver**

Silver can move fast, very fast.

Silver is:

- More volatile
- More speculative
- More sensitive to industrial cycles

This makes silver ideal for:

- Traders
- Long-term stackers seeking bigger gains
- Preppers needing barter metal

But less ideal for:

- Large wealth preservation
- Long-term sovereign storage

Gold tends to be:

- More stable
- More predictable
- Better suited for concentrated wealth

This is why most families seeking generational protection favor gold-heavy portfolios.

## Industrial Demand: Silver's Secret Engine

Unlike gold, silver is consumed in industry.

Silver is essential for:

- Solar panels
- Electronics
- Medical devices
- Batteries
- 5G and 6G infrastructure
- Water purification
- Robotics
- Military and defense applications

Many of these uses permanently destroy silver, shrinking global supply. This dual nature, monetary and industrial, explains why silver often explodes during shortages or technological booms.

## Storage Reality: Gold Is Efficient, Silver Is Bulky

Gold and silver differ not only in price and volatility, but also in how easily they can be stored and transported. Because silver is inexpensive per ounce, storing large value requires space.

For example:

- $100,000 in gold fits in your hand
- $100,000 in silver has a tangible heft

This is why vaulting or using offsite storage becomes important for large silver positions.

Gold is the king of value density, making it ideal for stealth wealth, portability, and mobility.

## Tactical Uses for Gold and Silver in a Crisis

In crisis environments, gold and silver serve distinct but complementary roles. Understanding how each metal functions during periods of disruption helps preserve wealth, maintain liquidity, and support practical decision-making when normal financial systems falter.

**Gold During Crisis:**

- Moves wealth across borders quietly
- Buys large assets (land, vehicles, relocation, opportunity)
- Acts as a final store of purchasing power
- Shields against inflation and currency resets

**Silver During Crisis:**

- Enables barter for food, fuel, medicine
- Functions as daily currency when fiat fails
- Remains recognizable even without special tools
- Facilitates small, fair transactions

In extreme scenarios, silver feeds the family; gold moves the family. Together, they preserve both continuity and flexibility.

## Crisis Hierarchy of Use

In periods of systemic breakdown, a natural hierarchy emerges:

Silver moves first. It circulates rapidly. It solves immediate problems: food, fuel, medicine, and local trade. Gold moves later. It addresses larger decisions: relocation, major assets, rebuilding, and long-term security.

Understanding this hierarchy prevents waste. Spending gold for small needs sacrifices strategic power. Hoarding silver without gold limits future mobility. Each metal has a purpose. Respecting that purpose protects financial independence and supports long-term autonomy.

## The Spiritual and Psychological Difference

Gold symbolizes stability, legacy, and deep time. Holding it feels like touching history, a bridge between past and future generations. Silver symbolizes activity, energy, and adaptability. It feels alive, dynamic, almost electric. Together, they form a complete defensive and offensive monetary strategy.

## Portfolio Strategy: The Traditional and Tactical Mix

Building resilience with precious metals is not simply about owning gold or silver, but about understanding how each metal contributes to a balanced and adaptable strategy.

**Most long-term wealth stewards choose:**

- 80% gold
- 20% silver

**Why? Because:**

- Gold preserves wealth and offers security
- Silver amplifies gains and provides leverage

When combined, they create a resilient shield against inflation, debt collapse, and digital currency restrictions.

Gold and silver are more than metals; they are a map of how humanity navigates crisis.

- Gold reminds you to stay grounded
- Silver reminds you to stay adaptable

As the world drifts toward digital money, surveillance, and debt implosion, these metals keep you grounded in truth, clarity, and self-reliance.

Where paper fails, metals outlast. Where systems collapse, metals survive. Where uncertainty rises, metals shine.

Your decision to understand the dance between gold and silver places you far ahead of the average investor and far better prepared to weather the storms ahead.

**For a deeper exploration of silver and practical acquisition strategies:**

*925 Thrift: The Pocket Guide To Finding Silver*

Your treasure map to zero in on undiscovered silver.

Available on Amazon in eBook and paperback formats.
Palmetto Publishing © 2023

Bring Your Sunblock

# The End Game

*Get busy living, or get busy dying.*
*Shawshank Redemption*

### "The Winter With No Power"

The ice storm came on fast, the kind of cold that numbs your fingers even indoors. By nightfall, the power went out. Then the cell towers. Then the stores closed. The world shrank into a quiet, frozen neighborhood where cash registers, credit cards, and digital systems suddenly meant nothing.

For the first time, I felt the unease of dependency and how fragile modern life truly is.

But I wasn't helpless. I lit candles, fired up the small generator I kept *"just in case,"* and rationed the supplies I had quietly stocked over the years. I reassured my family that everything would be okay, even though fear tugged at me.

In my lockbox were those small gold and silver pieces. In that silent, powerless winter, they looked like hope forged in metal.

Neighbors came to me for help, and I shared what I could. I didn't panic; I led.

By the time the power finally returned a week later, I realized something profound. Readiness isn't paranoia. It is foresight, resolve, and the ability to stay calm when pressure arrives.

That winter taught me a truth I will never forget:

In chaos, the ready become the helpers, not the victims.

## Endings Are Quiet at First

The end of a monetary system rarely announces itself with chaos. It begins administratively with policy adjustments, emergency measures, and temporary rules that quietly become permanent. Limits are imposed. Exceptions are normalized. Access becomes conditional.

What changes first is not daily life, but the range of choices available to individuals. Options narrow, flexibility fades, and dependence increases. This is how systems conclude, not with collapse, but with compression.

Gold matters in this phase because it expands choice precisely when structures begin to restrict it.

Every Fourth Turning is marked by upheaval and renewal. Old systems fail, and new foundations emerge. The Great Financial Reset is the monetary expression of this generational cycle: a culmination of excessive debt, institutional decay, economic fragility, and digital transformation.

We are not witnessing random chaos. We are witnessing the predictable climax of a historical cycle. Human civilization has entered a period of profound transition: economic, political, technological, and philosophical. The old monetary order is cracking under the weight of debt, inflation, digital overreach, and declining trust in institutions.

This chapter is where everything converges: gold, readiness, ownership over your future, and the courage to thrive even when structures falter. This is not a chapter about fear. This is a chapter about empowerment.

## The End Game: What It Means and Why It Matters

Every monetary system in history has an end. Not because people stop working or creating, but because governments:

- Spend more than they earn
- Print more than they can justify
- Inflate more than the public can endure
- Promise more than they can deliver

Eventually, the debt becomes too heavy, the currency too weak, and public trust too thin.

Systems fail slowly at first, then suddenly.

In this environment, those who position early tend to retain options when others lose them.

## Survival vs. Continuity

Most people prepare to survive disruption. Few plan for what comes after. Survival focuses on getting through hardship. Continuity focuses on preserving position once order returns.

Gold plays a unique role here. It does not just protect during breakdown; it preserves purchasing power for reconstruction.

After every reset, assets are redistributed. Those who preserved real value acquire what others lost. This is not exploitation. It is arithmetic.

Continuity belongs to those who thought ahead.

## The Crack-Up Boom: The Final Stage of a Dying Currency

A crack-up boom is the final phase of a failing monetary system, when confidence in the currency collapses and people rush to exchange money for tangible goods. The concept, described by economist Ludwig von Mises, refers to the moment when inflation expectations spiral and the public abandons money in favor of real assets.

A crack-up boom occurs when:

- The public loses faith in currency
- People rush to convert money into anything real
- Inflation accelerates uncontrollably
- Governments print more, worsening conditions
- Prices soar as trust collapses

This is not hypothetical. History provides several examples:

- Weimar Germany
- Zimbabwe
- Argentina (multiple times)
- Venezuela
- The Roman Empire

Many historical fiat systems have followed this pattern.

Gold stands outside this loop, untouched by inflation, panic, and political games. Gold is the lifeboat when the monetary ship begins to sink.

## Prepping: The Art of Peaceful Readiness

Prepping is not about bunkers, and it is not about fear. It is about responsibility, clear thinking, and the ability to act when others hesitate.

A prepper is not someone waiting for disaster. A prepper is someone who refuses to depend on unstable dependencies.

### 1. Financial Preparedness

Gold becomes the backbone of resilience. It preserves purchasing power. It cannot be frozen or seized digitally. It moves with you. It protects during currency collapse.

### 2. Physical Preparedness

Gold cannot purify water or heat a home, which is why preparedness includes:

- Food reserves
- Clean water systems
- Energy backups

- Medical supplies
- Essential tools

The goal is not fear; the goal is freedom.

## 3. Essential Skills

In an end-game environment, skills become currency:

- Repair
- First aid
- Gardening
- Bartering
- Negotiation
- Tactical awareness
- Self-protection competencies
- Community leadership

## Barter and Exchange: Silver for Today, Gold for Tomorrow

During monetary breakdowns, a natural hierarchy develops.

Silver is ideal for:

- Food
- Fuel
- Clothing
- Local trade
- Small transactions

Gold is ideal for:

- Relocation
- Large purchases
- Securing safety

- Preserving family wealth
- Rebuilding after collapse

Silver keeps the household running. Gold preserves the family's future.

## Global Mobility: The Strategic Secret Few Understand

During Fourth Turning crises:

- Borders tighten
- Capital controls emerge
- Governments panic
- Citizens suffer the consequences

Gold, especially in small, discreet forms, provides portable wealth, border-crossing mobility, global liquidity, and autonomy without permission.

Throughout history, families survived wars, persecutions, and political collapses because they held gold. Gold was not just wealth; it was freedom.

## Leadership Through Preparation

In crisis, prepared individuals become anchors for others. Composure spreads. Resources stabilize communities. Leadership emerges not through authority, but through readiness.

Those who plan ahead do not panic; they maintain options and act with intention. That difference matters.

Gold does not isolate people. It empowers them to help without becoming dependent themselves. In crisis, those who are ready naturally become the ones others turn to for help.

The end game rewards foresight. It punishes complacency. It remembers who remained capable when systems faltered.

## Wealth Sovereignty: The Core Principle

As governments implement digital identification, financial surveillance, and CBDCs, freedom becomes increasingly linked to compliance. Gold offers one way to step outside this chain.

Gold is:

- Uninflatable
- Uncensorable
- Untrackable
- Unprogrammable

It is private wealth in physical form.

As digital networks tighten around the individual, gold stands alone as freedom you can touch.

## Protection Against Systemic Risk

Modern society depends on fragile infrastructure:

- Electrical grids
- Payment networks
- Internet infrastructure
- Supply chains
- Bank liquidity

Failure of even one critical link can spread chaos quickly.

Gold protects against several systemic risks:

- Bank failures
- Bail-ins
- Bail-outs
- Capital and credit freezes
- Inflation shocks

- Digital outages
- Political asset seizures

Maintaining optionality becomes the real advantage.

## The Psychology of Being Prepared

Preparation changes more than circumstances; it transforms the way you think, decide, and respond when systems begin to strain.

Ready individuals experience:

- Less fear
- More confidence
- Stronger families
- Better decision-making
- Greater peace of mind

Readiness transforms uncertainty into opportunity. It shifts your mindset from reactive to strategic. Instead of worrying about what could go wrong, you focus on what you can influence. Your mindset becomes your greatest asset.

In the end game of a failing monetary system, you face two choices:

- Depend on collapsing institutions
- Become your own institution

Gold is not merely a hedge. Gold is a declaration:

*"I refuse to be at the mercy of failing institutions."*

Preparedness is not retreat. Preparedness is rising above. As the world drifts toward digital money, heavy-handed governments, and economic instability, those who position early will not only survive...

They will lead the way into the new era.

# Nuggets

*What we do in life echoes in eternity.*
*Gladiator*

Gold becomes more than a metal. Over time, it becomes a mindset, a way of thinking that favors responsibility, patience, and long-term perspective. It is not only about what you own, but about who you become along the way.

## Gold as a Long-Term Discipline

Gold rewards behavior more than timing. Those who accumulate steadily outperform those who speculate aggressively. Those who hold patiently outperform those who trade emotionally. Gold favors consistency, restraint, and long-term thinking in a world addicted to immediacy.

Gold does not demand constant attention. It does not react to headlines. It does not tempt over-activity. Instead, it teaches discipline by doing nothing at all.

This quiet discipline compounds beyond finance. It shapes decision-making, patience, and self-control, qualities that strengthen every area of life.

Gold is not a shortcut; it is a commitment.

## Golden Nuggets

These are not merely tips; they are distilled truths learned across centuries, through crises, collapses, rebuilds, and generations of human experience. Each principle reflects lessons repeated throughout history by those who understood how real wealth is preserved.

## 1. Buy Consistently, Calmly, Quietly

Wealth is not built in moments of frenzy. It's built in steady accumulation A monthly gram beats an occasional ounce. Consistency beats intensity.

## 2. Focus on Weight, Not Shine

Beware of high-premium collectibles (unless you're a numismatist). Your goal is wealth density: ounces, grams, purity. Shiny designs do not store wealth. Gold content does.

## 3. Avoid Emotional Selling

Markets dip. Beginners panic. Veterans buy. As trust fades, gold rises. Selling your gold emotionally is like selling your parachute midair.

## 4. Keep Your Circle Small

Your wealth is safest when only you control the narrative. Silence is a strategy. Discretion protects not only your assets, but your personal security.

## 5. Trust the Metal, Not the Markets

Markets fluctuate. Governments change. Currencies weaken. Gold simply is.

## Never Sell, Borrow Instead: The Strategy of the Wealthy

One of the enduring strategies of generational wealth is this: the wealthy rarely sell their gold; they borrow against it. By using gold as collateral rather than liquidating it, they preserve the asset while still gaining access to liquidity when needed.

**Why? Because:**

## Selling Gold:

- Triggers taxes
- Decreases long-term wealth
- Removes your inflation hedge
- Breaks the compounding cycle

## Borrowing Against Gold:

- Preserves your holdings
- Gives immediate liquidity
- Avoids capital gains taxes in many regions
- Allows strategic reinvestment
- Maintains your asset base for the next generation

This is how dynasties think.

Their goal is not to "cash out." Their goal is to never run out.

When you borrow against gold, you maintain ownership of your past while accessing resources for your future. It is the perfect blend of defense and offense.

## Preserving the Base

Selling gold should be a last resort. Once sold, it rarely returns.

Borrowing against gold when done prudently allows liquidity without sacrificing long-term security. This approach separates consumption from stewardship and preserves the asset base across generations.

Wealth is not built by liquidation. It is built by preservation.

Those who understand this distinction maintain continuity through disruption while others reset repeatedly. Gold works best when it remains untouched.

## "The Unbreakable Lesson"

My hardest chapter began quietly. A sudden job loss. Bills piling up. Unexpected expenses. Sleepless nights. I tried to stay strong, but the pressure grew heavier each week. Even my confidence began to crack.

There were moments, dark ones, when giving up felt easier than fighting.

But I remembered the stories:

My grandmother's basement safe...
The coin shop owner who guided me...
The winter storm where preparedness carried my family through...

Every chapter of my life had been teaching me resilience. So, I chose something simple, but powerful: I started rebuilding, slowly and deliberately.

I devised and began working a well-calculated plan as described in *925 Thrift: The Pocket Guide To Finding Silver*.

One small act of sovereignty at a time. The treasure hunt was on. A little silver here. A little gold there.

Saving felt like reclaiming agency. Learning felt like reclaiming power. Growing felt like reclaiming dignity.

Months passed. Then years. I worked my way back, stronger, wiser, and calmer. One day I looked around at my life and realized something. Nothing was the same, especially me.

I didn't just survive the failures of the system I transcended them.

## Family Wealth Building: The Art of Multi-Generational Resolve

Gold is the ultimate generational asset. It does not decay, corrode, or disappear. It is wealth that transcends eras.

But family wealth is not measured only in ounces.

It is built through:

- Knowledge
- Habits
- Values
- Planning
- Resilience
- Responsibility
- Love

By building a gold position and teaching your family why, you pass on more than money; you pass on mindset.

## Building a Family Tradition

Families who succeed across generations do the following:

### ✓ Teach Children Early

Explain gold simply: "This is money that never dies."

### ✓ Create a Documented Family Plan

Where it's stored, how to access it, and what it's for.

### ✓ Set Rules for Its Use

Gold is reserved for emergencies, major opportunities, and generational legacy, not for impulse purchases or short-term spending.

### ✓ Tell the Stories

Your grandmother's safe.
Your first silver swap.
The winter storm.

The rebirth after financial hardship.
The last gift...

Emotional stories become the glue that binds generations around shared wisdom.

### ✓ Model the Behavior

Your discipline becomes their inheritance.

## Legacy Is Built Quietly

Most legacies are invisible while they are being built.

Gold sits quietly while currencies weaken, markets surge and crash, and policies shift. It does not demand validation. It does not seek applause. It simply remains.

Passing gold forward is not about inheritance alone; it is about transmitting mindset, discipline, and the habits that sustain wealth across generations.

## The Emotional Return on Gold

Beyond price movements or portfolio performance, gold delivers something stocks, crypto, and paper money cannot:

- Peace of mind

Gold:

- Provides psychological stability
- Reduces financial anxiety
- Restores self-reliance
- Encourages long-term thinking

When the world grows chaotic economically, politically, technologically, gold becomes a psychological refuge.

The simple act of holding it reminds you:

*"I am not powerless."*

## A Positive Closing Message: Hope in an Uncertain World

Yes — the monetary order is under strain.
Yes — the debt bubble is expanding and about to pop.
Yes — governments are moving toward digital control.
Yes — inflation is eroding purchasing power.
Yes — the old world is dissolving.

But here is the truth:

You are not required to dissolve with it.

Gold represents the part of you that survives every transition, every storm, every systemic failure. It is the symbol of endurance, courage, preparation, intelligence, self-respect, and hope.

Gold does not just preserve wealth; it preserves possibility.

You are building something powerful, something your family will thank you for long after you're gone.

You are creating:

✔ **A legacy**

✔ **A foundation**

✔ **A protective fortress around your future**

And you are doing it in a world where few have the wisdom or fortitude to plan ahead.

That alone makes you part of a rare group, one that not only survives upheaval, but emerges from it stronger.

# R&R

*Let's hug it out b\*tch.*
*Entourage*

For readers who want to go further on their journey toward financial resilience and sovereignty, the following books and voices provide essential perspective. They expand your understanding of monetary history, generational cycles, crisis navigation, psychology, and the enduring role of precious metals.

Together, these works extend the ideas explored in this guide and equip you with the wisdom, context, and tools needed to navigate the Great Financial Reset with confidence and clarity.

## Recommended Books:

• *925 Thrift: The Pocket Guide To Finding Silver* — R.E. Gold
Practical, empowering methods for locating real-world silver at discounted prices.

• *1984* — George Orwell
Orwell's stark warning about a future dominated by surveillance of every thought, censorship, fear, propaganda, and unrelenting authoritarianism.

• *Gold: The Once and Future Money* — Nathan Lewis
A compelling exploration of why gold has anchored stable monetary systems throughout history and its essential place in tomorrow's economy.

• *The New Case for Gold* — James Rickards
A powerful argument for the necessity of gold in modern portfolios.

• *When Money Dies* — Adam Fergusson
A firsthand look at hyperinflation in Weimar Germany. Required reading for understanding crack-up booms.

- *Human Action* — Ludwig von Mises
A profound exploration of how individual choices shape markets, advocating for free-market economics and critiquing government intervention.

- *The Creature from Jekyll Island* — G. Edward Griffin
A dramatic, revealing history of the Federal Reserve and fiat money.

- *Fed Up* — Danielle DiMartino Booth
An insider's take on why the Federal Reserve is bad for America.

- *The Road to Serfdom* — F.A. Hayek
A powerful warning about government overreach and the economic consequences of centralized control.

- *The Fourth Turning* — William Strauss and Neil Howe
The foundational text on generational cycles and crisis eras.

- *The Black Swan* — Nassim Nicholas Taleb
Understanding the impact of rare, unexpected events.

- *Atomic Habits* — James Clear
For building disciplined, sovereign habits that compound into security.

- *Meditations* — Marcus Aurelius
Timeless lessons in self-mastery during times of uncertainty.

- *The Art of War* — Sun Tzu
Timeless strategies and leadership principles that apply to modern business, leadership, and strategy, focusing on breaking resistance without fighting.

- *The 48 Laws of Power* — Robert Greene
A comprehensive guide distilling 3,000 years of power dynamics into 48 essential laws, drawing from historical figures and philosophers to teach strategies for gaining and maintaining control.

## Recommended YouTube Influencers:

- 2is1gold
- Alasdair Macleod
- Andy Schectman
- Bald Guy Money
- Bill Holter
- David Morgan
- Frank Giustra
- George Gammon
- ITM Trading
- J Bravo
- Jeremiah Babe
- Jim Rickards
- Joe Rogan
- KITCO
- Liberty & Finance
- Lynette Zang
- Maneco64
- Mark Moss
- Michael Oliver
- Miles Franklin Media
- Peter Schiff
- Rafi Farber
- Rick Rule
- Ron's Basement
- SD Bullion
- YANKEE Stacking

## "The Last Gift"

Years ago, when my grandmother fell ill, I spent evenings sitting by her bedside listening to stories: tales of hardship, war-times, migration, inflation, and the quiet battles previous generations fought without fanfare.

One evening, she handed me a small leather pouch. Inside were gold coins, worn, scarred, and full of life.

*"This is not wealth,"* she said softly. *"This is a message."*

She explained that true wealth isn't measured in ounces. It's measured in wisdom, resilience, and the strength to stay independent as institutions rise and fall.

In a world drifting toward digital surveillance, programmable money, and a financial structure that feels increasingly Orwellian, that small pouch became my anchor.

It reminded me of something simple and powerful:

Generations before me survived storms I will never know. We will survive the storms ahead.

And one day, I will pass down my own coin pouch, a legacy cache to my children, not just metal, but of lessons, love, resilience, and self-reliance.

# Terminology

## A

**Agency**: The capacity to act intentionally and make independent choices in pursuit of personal stability and long-term resilience.

**Allocated Storage**: A storage method where specific gold bars or coins are assigned directly to the owner. You own the exact items stored, not a pooled or fractional claim.

**Autonomy**: The ability to maintain independent control over one's financial decisions, resources, and future without relying entirely on external institutions or systems.

**Awakening (Second Turning)**: A generational phase characterized by cultural change, spiritual questioning, and societal re-evaluation.

## B

**Barter**: Trading goods or services directly without currency. Gold and silver historically function as barter tools during instability.

**Basement Safe (Metaphorical)**: A symbol of early financial sovereignty representing the first lesson in self-storage and tangible wealth ownership.

**Big Brother**: A reference to growing digital surveillance, tracking, and financial monitoring inspired by George Orwell's novel, *1984*.

**Bullion**: High-purity physical gold or silver in coins, bars, or rounds purchased primarily for investment.

# C

**Capital Controls**: Government-imposed restrictions on the movement, withdrawal, or conversion of money.

**Central Bank**: The authority that manages a nation's currency, money supply, and interest rates.

**Crack-Up Boom**: The final phase of a failing currency system where excessive money printing triggers panic buying of real assets.

**Crisis Phase**: Within the framework of The Fourth Turning, this is the period when long-running monetary distortions reach their limits, forcing a reckoning in currency, debt, and trust, followed by the construction of a new financial order.

**Currency**: A medium of exchange used as money.

**Currency Devaluation**: The loss of a currency's purchasing power due to inflation or monetary expansion.

# D

**Debt Bubble**: When government, corporate, or household debt grows so large that collapse becomes inevitable.

**Digital Currency (CBDC)**: Programmable, trackable, and fully monitored digital money.

**Durability (Gold Property)**: Gold's resistance to corrosion and decay, contributing to its long-term value.

# E

**Economic Sovereignty**: Control over one's wealth independent of banks, governments, or digital platforms.

**End Game (Financial)**: The final stage of a monetary system marked by hyperinflation, loss of trust, and systemic restructuring.

**Era of Crisis (Fourth Turning)**: The generational period characterized by upheaval, institutional collapse, and rebuilding.

# F

**Fiat Currency**: Government-issued money not backed by physical assets.

**Fractional Gold/Silver Coins**: Small denominations (1/10 oz, 1g, 5g) used for barter or emergency liquidity.

**Fourth Turning**: The final generational phase described by Strauss and Howe, a period of crisis leading to system-wide transformation.

# G

**Gilded Wealth**: Wealth built not only on metals but on discipline, foresight, and preparation.

**Global Debt Bomb**: Worldwide debt levels that have grown so large and unstable that even small economic shocks can trigger cascading defaults, currency failures, or systemic collapse.

**Gold-to-Silver Ratio (GSR)**: The number of ounces of silver equal to the value of one ounce of gold, serving as a long-standing indicator of relative valuation, monetary stress, and capital flows between the two metals.

**Gresham's Law**: "Bad money drives out good money." People save gold and spend weakening fiat.

# H

**Hard Assets**: Tangible, real assets like gold, silver, or land.

**Hedge**: To reduce financial risk by holding an asset that gains value when another loses value.

**Heirloom Wealth**: Wealth passed through generations in durable, tangible, physical form.

# I

**Inflation**: An abnormal increase in the volume of money and credit resulting in the substantial and continuing rise in the general price level.

**Intrinsic Value**: The inherent, fundamental worth of an asset, based on its underlying qualities, utility, and objective characteristics, rather than its current market price or speculative demand.

# J

**Jurisdictional Risk**: The risk associated with storing wealth in unstable or intrusive political environments.

# K

**Karat (K)**: A measure of gold purity.

# L

**Liquidity**: Ease with which an asset can be converted to cash or goods.

# M

**Macro-Economic Instability**: Large-scale economic stress such as inflation, recession, or currency weakness.

**Mintage**: The production of coins, particularly those intended as bullion.

**Money**: A medium of exchange and store of value used to facilitate trade.

# N

**Neodymium Rare Earth Magnet**: Made from an alloy of neodymium, iron, and boron to form a tetragonal crystalline structure. A powerful permanent magnet available commercially to test for magnetism and verify authenticity.

**Nugget**: Something of great value or significance; in the context of precious metals, it refers to gold in its most elemental, unrefined form, scarce and independent of monetary systems.

**Numismatics**: The study or collection of coins valued for rarity rather than metal content.

# O

**Orwellian**: Situations, systems, or behaviors that reflect the oppressive, manipulative, or dystopian themes found in George Orwell's works.

**Overreach (Government)**: Expansion of government power into private financial and personal domains.

**Overshoot Phase (Fourth Turning)**: The moment in crisis when systems push past their sustainable limits.

# P

**Pooled Storage**: Storage where metals are combined with other clients' holdings.

**Prepping**: Preparing for disruptions through skills, supplies, and resilient wealth.

**Purity**: The measure of gold content within an item, typically expressed as a decimal such as .999 or .9999, indicating 99.9% or 99.99% pure gold.

# Q

**Quantitative Easing (QE)**: Central bank policy of printing new money to stimulate the economy.

# R

**Rehypothecation**: Using someone else's pledged assets as collateral.

**Resilience (Financial)**: The ability to withstand disruption through preparation.

**Reset (Financial)**: Large-scale restructuring of currency, debt, and institutions, central to the Great Financial Reset.

# S

**Safe Haven Asset**: An asset that retains value during crisis.

**Segregated Storage**: Vaulting where metals are stored separately and labeled for the owner.

**Sovereignty**: The power to govern oneself without outside interference.

**Strauss and Howe Generational Theory**: A historical framework describing recurring 80 to 100-year societal cycles.

# T

**Tangible Wealth**: Physical assets such as metals or land.

**Turning (Generational)**: One of the four phases in Strauss and Howe cycles.

# U

**Unallocated Gold**: Gold held on paper without a specific physical bar assigned.

# V

**Vaulting Partner (Private Vault)**: A private entity offering secure, insured metal storage outside traditional banking.

# W

**Wealth Preservation**: Protecting purchasing power over long time periods.

**Wearable Wealth:** Portable stores of intrinsic value designed to be worn on the body.

**Winter Crisis (Metaphorical)**: The harsh phase of a societal or financial cycle, synonymous with the Fourth Turning.

# Z

**Zero Counterparty Risk**: When an asset requires no third party promise to retain value, such as gold and silver.

# Appendix

## Understanding The Fourth Turning & The Great Financial Reset

### What Is the Fourth Turning?

The Fourth Turning, as described by William Strauss and Neil Howe, is the final phase in a recurring historical cycle. Each cycle lasts 80–100 years and consists of four distinct turnings: growth, awakening, unraveling, and crisis. The Fourth Turning is the crisis phase, the moment when institutions fail, trust collapses, and society undergoes a necessary transformation.

Throughout history, Fourth Turnings have included:

- The American Revolution
- The Civil War
- The Great Depression & World War II

Each crisis shattered old institutions and gave birth to new structures. Each created hardship but also opportunity. Each demanded courage, preparation, and leadership. We are in such a cycle now.

### What Is the Great Financial Reset?

The Great Financial Reset is the economic expression of this crisis phase. It is driven by converging structural pressures, including:

- Exploding global debt
- Currency devaluation
- Inflation and capital erosion
- Overreliance on money printing
- Declining trust in institutions
- Rising digital surveillance
- CBDC initiatives and programmable money

These forces make the existing framework unsustainable. Eventually, the financial order must reset through currency reform, debt restructuring, or systemic overhaul.

## How the Two Intersect

The Fourth Turning describes **why** institutions collapse. The Great Financial Reset describes **how** the monetary order collapses.

Together, they reveal why:

- Governments are expanding control
- Inflation is accelerating
- Currencies are weakening
- Societal tension is rising

These developments are not random. They are signals of a historical cycle reaching its climax.

## Why Gold Matters in This Moment

During Fourth Turnings and financial resets, gold becomes vital because it:

- Exists outside digital constraints
- Preserves purchasing power
- Protects against inflation
- Provides continuity through currency reform
- Maintains wealth when institutions fail

## A Final Message…

We are living through a historic transition. But transitions are not merely endings; they are beginnings. By understanding the cycles, preparing wisely, and anchoring wealth in assets like gold and silver, you position yourself not just to endure the Fourth Turning and Great Financial Reset, but to emerge from it more resilient, more independent, and undeniably sovereign.

# Acknowledgments

I am grateful to my children, Ari and Gianni, whose future reinforces the responsibility to think for ourselves, act deliberately, and prepare wisely. They motivate me daily to remain curious, vigilant, and committed to readiness in an uncertain world.

I would also like to acknowledge the many independent educators, analysts, and content creators who have shared their knowledge over the years. Through countless hours of research, discussion, and education, you have helped illuminate complex financial realities and empowered others to think critically, prepare strategically, and take responsibility for their financial futures.

# About the Author

R. E. Gold was born and raised in Upstate New York, shaped by the values of a close-knit Italian family where tradition, self-reliance, and respect were woven into daily life. Growing up during what he considers a fortunate and formative time, he developed a deep appreciation for learning, hard work, and personal responsibility.

His academic interests span engineering, economics, biology, ecology, and the culinary arts, reflecting a lifelong curiosity about how systems — natural, financial, and human — interact. Extensive travel and exposure to diverse cultures further shaped his understanding of the world and broadened his perspective. Grounded by music, nature, lifelong friendships, and a strong extended family, he approaches each new day with gratitude and the belief that every tomorrow holds opportunity.

R. E. Gold is a best-selling author focused on precious metals, wealth preservation, and financial self-reliance. His previous book, *925 Thrift: The Pocket Guide To Finding Silver*, was published by Palmetto Publishing in 2023.

Continue the journey with *925 Thrift: The Pocket Guide To Finding Silver*, available on Amazon in eBook and paperback.

"Gold is money. Everything else is credit."

—J.P. Morgan 1912

www.ingramcontent.com/pod-product-compliance
Lightning Source LLC
LaVergne TN
LVHW010404070526
838199LV00065B/5893